THE LISTENING SKIN

Also by Glenis Redmond

Backbone
Under the Sun
What My Hand Say
Praise Songs for Dave the Potter, Art by Jonathan Green and Poetry
by Glenis Redmond

The Listening Skin

Glenis Redmond

Four Way Books
Tribeca

for my mama, Jeanette Redmond
for my daughters, Celeste Sherer Farmand and Amber Sherer
for my grandchildren, Julian Priester and Paisley Farmand
for the ancestors
for myself
and all HSPs (Highly Sensitive Persons)
may you find a soft place to land in these words and in the world

Library of Congress Cataloging-in-Publication Data

Names: Redmond, Glenis, author.
Title: The listening skin / Glenis Redmond.
Description: [New York] : Four Way Books, [2022] | Identifiers: LCCN 2022003863 |
ISBN 9781954245259 (paperback) | ISBN
9781954245372 (epub)
Subjects: LCGFT: Poetry.
Classification: LCC PS3618.E4347 L56 2022 | DDC 811/.6--dc23
LC record available at https://lccn.loc.gov/2022003863

This book is manufactured in the United States of America and printed on
acid-free paper.

Four Way Books is a not-for-profit literary press. We are grateful for the assistance
we receive from individual donors, public arts agencies, and private foundations
including the NEA, NEA Cares, Literary Arts Emergency Fund, and the
New York State Council on the Arts, a state agency.

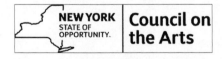

PROUD MEMBER

[clmp]

We are a proud member of the Community of Literary Magazines and Presses.

Contents

Flashback

Flight

Sometimes the skin seems to be the best listener, as it prickles and thrills, say to a sound or a silence; or the fantasy, the imagination: how it bursts into inner pictures as it listens and then responds by pressing its language, its forms, into the listening clay. To be open to what we hear, to be open in what we say.

MC Richards

listen,
you a wonder.
you a city of a woman.
you got a geography
of your own.

Lucille Clifton

Afro Carolinian

after Sean Hill

With Carolina on my lips, I sing a quilt,
a crooked stitch that weaves its way around
my pie-shaped state that conjures food—
too sweet like amber iced tea or cake, red-velvet rich.
Too sweet, like the words I was raised on, words that say,
If you don't have nothin nice to say,   *lace it with sugah.*
There's always more in the South, like the twos and threes
coming out of grandma's mouth, *Hush your mouth, chile.*
These words not a command for silence but a signal for the teller
to keep on spinning cause her words hit bone.
Grandma's words were codes—lit lanterns:
We gwine down yonder in the merrnin—
not a pronouncement to a destination
but a place where she'd teach a lesson
at her favorite fishing spot. By her foot,
a coffee can full of night crawlers,
in her mouth, a cigarette she barely puffed,
in her hands, a homemade fishing rod,
line steeped in the water waiting for hook tug.
She never said the word *patience*
just stood live oak–like,
grounded in her own wisdom,
a Baptist Buddha woman teaching
Be Here Now.

Her uncanny ways taught me
how to wait on the spirit.
Hunched in her favorite recliner,
King James Bible on the left—
her eyes forward, soaking in wrastlin.
Her faith rooted in the Lord and Ricky Steamboat.
I was rapt in how she'd contort herself,
as if she were head-locking demons,
choke-holding them in Jesus's name.
Simultaneously burning tufts of her hair in a glass ashtray,
raked from her comb, so no one could work a root.
Grandma taught me the truth was a complex helix rising.
From her I learned how to watch as well as pray,
and how the shackled speak in double tongues.
As second daughter of a second daughter, I began life
as a shame-faced girl too shy to string together words.
I did not open my mouth until I had something to say.
I was busy looking in grown folks' mouths,
collecting the old ways, placing them on my tongue.
My first language was scratched from the land:
sweet potatoes, collards, and black-eyed peas.
As a second daughter of a second daughter,
I straddle the abyss of the diaspora and the church pew,
where I learn to speak Afro Carolinian fluently.

Some call it a backwards tongue.
I call it a knowing, a spiritual
that will carry you forward
if you listen and learn how to sing it.

Flinch

Forefather

for David Drake,
enslaved potter-poet
from Edgefield, SC

When the landscape does not bear black blooms
I reach my arms back for one
who flares with instruction.
Read what he wrote on Edgefield pots:

"This is a noble churn |
fill it up it will never turn."

From my childhood home
a mere seventy-three miles' ragged stretch
from Piedmont to Edgefield separates us,
I make him out through one hundred and fifty-five years
through the muck and the fog of pale deceit.

I let my fingers touch his clay brilliance.
See him, a solid figure, a South Carolina son,
a Literary Father with no daguerreotype.
I conjure his visage
in both verse and vessel.
Through the whorls of his fingerprints
I walk along the loops and ridges,
sit between the lines of his etched couplets.
Press ear to the hum of hardened clay.

Hear him say, "Empty yourself.
Pry these tight spaces open.
Listen to the mountains and valleys
I withstood."

Make No Apologies for Yourself

Dear you, make no apologies for yourself
because you are covered in a listening skin
Because every ache you feel is not your own
Because of the bowl of sorrow your mother carries
Because of your father's wildfire moods
Because of how many rivers they crossed
Because of the lynching tree
Because when you enter bookstores
volumes fall off shelves into your open palms
Because you ask questions of the universe
and it answers and opens before you like a page
Because you can read the sky: those clouds
and that murder of crows
Because poets are your wounded idols
Because the truth even if it hurts
it is to be cherished and held
and just because people die
does not mean they do not walk with you daily
Because the river has a mouth that speaks their names
Because the river flows with stories
Because you sit on the shore and listen
Because alone is more comforting
than being together
Because your pen is oceanic

Because you are eyes wide
equipped with outer and inner sight
Because you suffer from what you see and hear
Because you have sinus arrhythmia and your breath is short
Because asthma is one of the monkeys on your back
Because your heart is the vehicle you choose to ride this go round
Because it can go forward and backwards in time
Because bookstores are your oracles
Because poetry is your greatest archeological tool
Because you plummet even though you can barely swim
Because you trust the ride of journal and journey
even if you do not always float
Because your heart beats to your breath
Because of this music you dance raw and wild

Mule

De nigger woman is de mule uh de world.
Zora Neale Hurston, *Their Eyes Were Watching God*

she scowls all the time   cause her shoulders bow underneath
work and worry   gets nothin in return   that's why she plants
her feet in a stubborn stance   that's why she don't move when
others around her say move   sometimes all a woman's got is her
push & pull against the grain   that's how she survives   how she
plods underneath the pack & load she carries   she carves out
rows   and with determined grit   if she likes you   you might get
a taste of her metallic wit flashing like silver starlight every now
and again   if she don't like you she will give you nothin but raised
hand and back-turned attitude   if you're wise you'll escape the eyes
the rapier-glare more serrated than words   if you're smart you'll
know better than to get into a kicking contest with a mule   you'll
see that she's had it tough in this world   the same world that will
never love her and see that she's a jewel   the same world who will
never recognize that black diamond gleam she brings   you know
what she knows   the world only wants her for her sweat step and
groan   that's why she keeps to her own clock cause she knows she
will never be fully realized or idealized not in this lifetime and she's
destined to die undervalued and overworked

From the Mouth of the River

for the Reedy River

I blame the sharp edges of your father
  who put the fight, flight, and fear into you.
    Every sight and sound magnified,
      so when you walk by me,
      my rush makes you look over your shoulder.
    Feel his hot breath. Lost in panic you check for footsteps.
    Your back is always turned to me.
        You judge me by your parents' lack: their inability to swim
          because Jim Crow laws barred their access to water—
            no swimming holes and pools for them.
          Grandma fished in lakes unafraid you say,
      but still you do not come to my edge,
      because you live so close to yours.
      You rarely dip a big toe.
        You refuse to stand still
          long enough to heal.
            I speak loud—
            in lashing rocks,
              not to scare you,
              but to let music tend
                to your brokenness.
              You've been traumatized
                by the Tallahatchie,
                  it roars the loudest to you.

Shaken to your core,
you hold history against me.
You keep Emmet Till's
bloated swell on playback.
What would I give for you
to lay your burdens down?
Trust I am not your enemy.
Only human hands taint me,
but your central nervous system is too
turned up
to receive what I offer: the hawk in her nest,
my rushing sounds echoing the Cherokee.
My ancient song heals.
If you stand still long enough,
you'll be in my flow.
Know. I don't take life.
I give it.

Mama Teaches Me How to Survive
by Teaching Me How to Dig My Own Grave

Not to throw blame, this is just to say
Mama taught me how to be a mule,
how to carry beyond a full load—
walk like *I don't feel no ways tired*, but I am.
I ran out of gas twenty years ago,
but I drove myself on sheer will and her words:
You don't have nothin to do?
I'll find you something to do.
I took on her ways to earn my keep.
I was on the lookout
for what needed to be done.
Knee bent, I scrubbed our kitchen floors
on my own 11-year-old volition.
Grew a garden from seed.
Hoed, raked, planted, and weeded,
cooked meals for a family of seven—
deemed the best babysitter of the village.
For one family, I cared for six boys,
their oldest was three years my elder,
but it was my charge they trusted.
For payment I bartered for an antique vanity.
Women's work they say is never done,
but I'm at my own end.
was raised to slave. I feel tired always.

The doctor diagnosis: *adrenal fatigue*
on top of fibromyalgia,
which sits on top of chronic fatigue,
which sits on top of irritable bowel,
which sits on top of leaky gut,
which sits on top of interstitial cystitis,
which sits on top of TMJ,
which sits on top of carpal tunnel,
which sits on top of multiple myeloma,
which is to say what Fannie Lou Hamer said,
I am sick and tired of being sick and tired.
I tote my Mama's, her Mama's, and her Mama's Mama loads.
Even in poetry, I push my pen
beyond the margins. Ride words hard
with a necessary and urgent pulse.
Put poems on my back,
carry their heavy weight
on pages and stages.
Slam them.
Found something to do
like my life depended on it.
I traded the mule in for a Mercedes.
Every one of those 340,000 miles, poetry miles.

First Do No Harm or How Not to See

Being called lazy throws me back
to the eighties to a trip downtown
with Mama for an appointment
with Dr. Griffin on Vardry Court.
Normally complaints of illness
in our house were met with, "You'll be alright."
This day, Mama took me seriously
after seeing how I suffered in silence
and how I contorted inward after every meal.
She witnessed how my back buckled as if whiplashed.
Mama was of the ilk who thought doctors'
words shone like pristine dictums.
Followed their instructions without question.
In the office, I tell the doctor what ails me.
After, he speaks only to Mama, "She's got one of those colons—
no matter what she swallows, even water it will cramp."
About her muscle pain—"nothing wrong with this girl, cept lazy."
His vacant laugh echoes.
I flash back to cotton fields and shackles
like Octavia Butler's Dana in *Kindred*.
I'm thrown to an imagined past,
instead of where I really stood,
a highly sought-after babysitter, a grocery store clerk,
summer hire at both 3M and Michelin,

President of the Junior class at Woodmont High School,
track star, who got up before dawn to practice
coming out the blocks faster,
a diligent daughter and a fluid dancer.
Mama and I leave the office never to return.
We both burn. We never speak of this transgression,
but I can feel Mama shapeshift into a caduceus.
Surround me with comfort and praise
as if to ward off the burgeoning heat of hate.

Medical History

On Mama's side the Todd men die young
no matter how early the sun goes up,
the women become bent from carrying their shadows.
In Waterloo, most of the white doctors
were steeped in a three-hundred-year-old belief
of black folks being chattel.
This backed by one hundred more years of separate,
but not nearly equal.
Uncle Pete age twenty-four
singed by the noonday sun,
drug his tired flesh from factory floor
to the colored-only side of the doctor's office,
with his throat swollen—his bones shuddering.
The doctor dispenses a cure for tonsillitis,
while ignoring Uncle Pete's documented diabetes.
The doctor orders him: "Go home, boy."
In a fever on the couch, he falls into a coma.
Slips away. His eyes never open to daylight again.

Blasphemy

Makes me want to shout
Isley Brothers

when black voices sing
and white bodies flail.
Mimic *the twist* or *the Watusi,*

acting out scenes from *Animal House*
or *Blues Brothers?* Both movies
cater to white frat-boy mentalities.

While they flail,
I flinch at the awkward
on-the-beat claps and stomps.

I cringe at this drunken party ritual
steeped in our gospel stories,
our rhythm and blues or just the blues,

the deepest hue of history.
At Erskine College I enter the cafeteria,
witness my first food fight.

I come from *ends that do not meet.*
I come from *waste not, want not.*
I come from *eat all you want but eat all you get.*

Not from African dance turned to sport
or food as folly or stomping carelessly on sacred ground.
In Carnegie Hall, the girl in room 107

informs me of what her Mama said,
"You can go to school with them,
but don't come back dancing all niggerish."

I metaphorically black out; when I come to,
I give her a piece of my father's temper.
I have read between every one of her *Gone with the Wind* lines.

I left the dance floor any time *Shout* played.
Don't get me wrong,
I love the Isley Brothers' R & B irreverence,
but I can't abide the blatant spectacle,
the sacrilege of white mimicry.

I sit this one out,
become a one-woman revolution.
I pray to accept the things that I cannot change
and the wisdom to raise my voice as a weapon.

In these classrooms:

I learn
I learn
I learn

to (shout) a little bit louder now
(shout) a little bit louder now
(shout) a little bit louder now

Mechanics of Muscle

In a clinch, I wonder if these wounds
carryover from a previous life:
rope around neck, body hung
hoisted and tree-strung.

My muscles stretch over my bones into a scream
as an invisible hand cranks
my jaw tighter than tight—
fastens my skull to shoulders,
raises neck to ears
into an upper-body clench,
a steel vice braces my head.
I can't turn left or right—
up or down.

I seek doctors and healers,
and they throw diagnoses on paper.
Prescribe pill after pill
I cannot even swallow,
because of dysphagia.

The chiropractor cracks my spine,
but my body does not obey,
bent on being unaligned.

In this locked cage I would complain,
but my mouth won't fully open,
words accompanied by pops and clicks,
the strange language of TMJ,
a distress call.

On the brink of bruxism
my teeth gnaw and gnash—
never do I deep sleep in this body.
It is its own torture device,
a cruel implement.

Every inch of me yells
when fibromyalgia flares.
How many times do I have to say uncle?
No matter how much
I twist, turn and croak:
I give I give
nothing does.

Out of Body

Out of my body is where I go,
when I can't bear being in it.

With its elephantine memory,
my body bears a psychic map

of every 'welt and wound.'
Sometimes

I fly out the window
with night wings.

From this height I can't feel
when bullets enter,

when the ax lands,
or when arrow-like words pierce.

On earth my body furls inward and weeps
like a wounded hawk.

The gunshots set off a chain.
Flash me back to a time when I was ten

and I slipped on the marble floor
outside my parents' bedroom.

My father fully dressed in camouflage fatigues
and combat boots stepped over me.

He never looked back—
out of the door he rushed to serve our country.

My father became a pain in my ass
that morning and remained one.

The same year the doctor asked my mother,
"Has your daughter sustained a blunt force trauma?

Her aches and pains present as a ninety-year-old woman."
The doctor prescribed a red rubber inner tube

for me to sit on at my desk in school,
as if I would add this insult to my injury

by making myself
a fifth-grade spectacle.

I forgive myself for falling,
but I don't forgive Dad's topple

off the pedestal I put him on. He slid in my eyes,
because he never put an arm out then or ever.

I became a tight fist,
an unbearable clench.

When most of my doctors say,
"Fibromyalgia is all in your head,"

my body says otherwise.
My cracked coccyx proves it.

Out of my body and out of my mind
is just where I am aiming to go:

to daydreams and thousand-yard stares
across stretches of land,

I travel where my father cannot touch me.
This is the only way

I inhabit here.

Meat Hook

With a muscular deftness,
invisible hands crank
and hoist my shoulders ear level,
to a place where it seems
every wrong I ever meted meets.
There they knot and quarrel.
They rive and rove,
as if a caliper entered the base
of my already stiff neck,
with an intentional grasp.
I let loose a shiver
The chill snakes beyond my control.
With my fingers,
I pulsate the mass. Masses.
They don't dissipate.
With meditation and intention,
I try to cut the cord psychically
—break the grip.
With Breath and Release,
I try to calm myself,
but I'm caught
by a high-handed hold
turning me from top to toe.
Never do I escape

this contortionist
twenty-eight-year tangle,
I think and dream
what a beautiful being
I would become
without this unbearable
thrashing of wings.

I Stay Sick

Mama says, *If it ain't one thing it's two.*
I was born half-baked & with a hernia at my core.
Sickness ran through & through me,
a red thread pinning one ailment to another.
I remember a friend once telling me,
"You've always been sickly."
Ever not see something in yourself until someone points it out?
She was right. I felt both ill & cursed
with my crooked spine. Fractured coccyx
and Osgood Schlatter limbs.
After every meal my colon contracted.
Our family knew nothing
about how healthy foods could be poison.
Lactose intolerant. Allium intolerant: Onion & garlic.
With IBS, I can't digest water. Everything swallowed
goes down like a stone. The Redmond Stomach
we call it. To be expected.
As a teenager I always had a throat full of white pus.
Strep-coated. Prescribed antibiotics for seven years.
Killed what little immunity I possessed.
When I was a young adult, the doctor finally removed
my tonsils. Twice. The second a sublingual set.
Allergies. Bronchitis in the spring.
Asthma. The cat must have stolen my breath

in the crib. Fainting spells. Vagal nerve response.

Menstrual flow like lava. Remove the uterus and ovaries.

Early menopause at age 37. Remove the gall bladder after an attack.

Pain a constant companion. Everywhere I go, she be.

In head. In throat. In stomach. In back. In ass. In knee. In feet.

Sieve for a bladder. Wrist riddled with electricity.

Carpal tunnel. Ulnar nerve damage. Fibromyalgia.

Finally, the big shoe drops, cancer.

Stage 3. Multiple myeloma.

I should have seen it coming. I didn't.

My daughter sends me Resilience, the ACEs,

the adverse childhood experience documentary

and quiz. She says, "I think you will find yourself in it."

I scored a 10. The research claims

adults with trauma-filled childhoods

will develop debilitating health issues. I concur.

When I go to the doctor, they hand me paperwork

with a chart to locate my pain. I can't pinpoint it.

I "X" my whole body. My entire life.

Fester

Tough Love Comes in the Dozens

We spit a 12-pack punch in full-tilt verbal throttle.
We slice the heart with tongue,
a sword fight where we battle with banter.
We train Cave Canem style.
Then, go off the chain to handle
this world in which we've been born.
We are passed through a hand-me-down *Soul Train* line rite of passage.
You better get in where you fit in. It's a rick-a-shay—*we got game*
—as we ping pong off the adrenaline on which we were all raised.

Our daddies and brothers carry us to barbershops, basketball
courts and street corners until we're fluent in trash talk
and high-top fades and fade aways. We spit insults
and throw the salt from our sweat in the wound.
We say, *It's all good in the hood, though we know it ain't and never will be.*

That's why we got game: We invented the cross over lay-up slam dunk
and created new ways, came back to show you how to play.
Check the kicks and the moves. Our tongues always fit the groove.
We got jokes that always begin with: *Yo Mama so black and ugly...*
when in doubt always insult the womb you come from,
as if we all didn't push off from that dark matter.

We're amnesiacs of our own origin story.
Don't take it personally or personal.
We step up by putting down—lame-ass lines don't fly.
We come from a straight-off-the-dome history.
Our metaphors be cooked in cotton fields,
fried in the sweat off our ancestors' backs.
Our tongue lashes are slave narrative–driven.
You better shoeshine those lines twelve times.
Remember your rhythm, son.
It's in the blood, the spit and the know Flow
Hood Code: *You's a pimp or you's being pimped.*
Cruel street don't take heed to Gandhi's
or Martin Luther King's middle ground.

We come from Malcolm X's *by any means necessary.*
We come from where Ali pummeled Lewis.
You better butterfly and bee sting it
with your fancy fist and fight dance.
Razzle dazzle them with your rope-a-dope,
bamboozle with your verse.
Stun 'em with your hip-hop wit.

We say, *It's all-good in the hood,*
though we know it ain't and never will be.
Why you think we be laughing while we crying?
We living in this devil-beating-his-wife rain.

Our world be half dozen in one and six in the other.
We combine the two, make our own truths
tap dance, even if it hurts.
This is our version of tough love.
We jab with jest. We got it like this:
Land street-fight blows with our mouths,
no rules, but each word we speak,
we make every syllable count.

A Partial Remembering of My History through Haiku

How I Learned to Dance and Read the Weather

> On eggshells I danced.
> Grooves to fit my father's moods.
> Tap dance. Bebop. Dirge.

Spin the Bottle All the Way Around

> Eleventh birthday.
> Only black girl in circle.
> Bottle lands on me.

> Eyes closed. Thick lips pursed.
> Chris used his shirt cuff as shield
> as if my black taints.

> My world spins backwards.
> I hold the hurt in my lungs.
> Right the world. Write it!

> Bring back my first kiss,
> a kind black boy with thick lips.
> In his eyes: mirrors.

1970's: Aviano, Italy, to Burlington, NJ, to Piedmont, SC

> White kids yell *nigger*
> as if the word's their birthright.
> I scowl all the time.

For a Colored Girl Who Considered Buying Hair Care
Products in Vermont When She Left Her Grease at Home

> Gurl, give up the ghost.
> You don't exist on their shelves.
> Seek relief elsewhere.

The Condition of My Heart or Why I Still Believe in the World

> My heart ain't broken:
> Rusted hinges stuck open
> It's congenital.

When Life Breaks You into Pieces, Make Yourself into a Quilt

> Take tatters in hand.
> Stitch. Sew patches of red clay.
> Plant feet on new ground.

Make America Better than It Has Been

Was our Again Great?
Ancestors beg to differ.
Our black life matters.

Ghosts

To say he ghosted me insults ghosts,
my haints linger in healing clusters.
When I need them most,
they drop a coin heads up,
leave a feather on my path,
flicker the streetlights
in a show of solidarity.
So, no he did not ghost me.
He did the most human thing—
left without explanation,
an intentional taking of my heart.
His silence, a violence,
a quiet war I battle
with someone I was coming to love.
His leaving suggests another side of him.
I don't always see with my eyeglasses tinted rose.
I don't always see red flags clearly.
Sometimes I think them decorations
for a parade.
With him, I'm left with an unknown,
but he did not ghost me.
My ghosts comfort,
they don't leave,
they cleave.

I Lost My Baby

Not in couldn't find, but in perished.
I lost my child
and still I was in search.
He found me in my bed busy dreaming.

I lost my child:
blond hair, hazel eyes, skin really fair.
He found me in my bed, busy dreaming.
He kissed me awake, though I was still asleep.

Blond hair, hazel eyes, skin really fair
shining like a familiar son.
He kissed me awake, though I was still asleep
saying, *I will tell Amber and Celeste there's no school, snow!*

Shining like a familiar sun,
how did he find us since we've moved three times?
He said, *Mom, I will tell Amber and Celeste there's no school, snow!*
Bedside you stood 12 years old, Cameron.

How did you find us since we've moved three times?
You stood bedside 12-years old, Cameron
with a quiet glow, *I am not lost, Mom I'm here. I'm still here.*

How I Summer (Read Simmer)

I feel most colored when I am thrown against a sharp white
background.
Zora Neale Hurston

I summer like bare feet on hot streets: uneasy.
On the beach I am hiding
as always in the pages of a book.
I am the Sesame Street song gone *wrong*.
One of these people is not like the other,
one of these people is not quite the same.
My heart, a bruised peach especially at Myrtle Beach.
Steeped in South Carolina's weighted history I keep reliving.
This snapshot in time does not capture how I got here.
Or, how I married white and into family vacations.
This is my first holiday at age twenty-nine.
Dressed in flip-flops and fuchsia Lycra.
I am black and blue collar uncomfortable.
I am from vacations never taken.
We played endless games of spades—
not going to the lake or amusement park rides.
We were in a tribe of *I. Declare. War.*
On school breaks we drank soda like water,
downed bags of Doritos and ran the streets
until the streetlamps came on. We busied ourselves
while our parents' worked minimum wage jobs. Vacation?
More like Vacation Bible School.
We made multi-colored God's eyes

from yarn and popsicle sticks.
We were quizzed on books of the bible.
I knew verses by rote: *God is our refuge and strength,*
and a very present help in trouble.
The Atlantic is beautiful, but troubled.
I am troubled too
even when I know
the sea holds healing salt.
My wounds resist.
I look up and out.
Instead of water,
I see acres of land,
black backs wavering,
curved like scythes.
Field hands they called us.
Our hands are made of fields.
I am red clay and cotton
especially at the water's edge.
Back on the beach,
I am overdressed.
Summer is hot in me.
I am full of this past present heat

I carry.
I come to the shore,
but I vacate nothing.

You Know You Are Not from Here

when your dad retires and announces *we're going home*
when South Carolina is just a concept not a place
when it would never dawn on your parents
to *preview* or *set the context* for the South
when they just load all six of you
into the 1974 puce green Chevy Nova
and head south on I-95
when you are eyes wide and full of questions
when you see a Sambo displayed on a roadside billboard
when as an Air Force child raised elsewhere
you do not understand the color lines
at basketball games or on Sunday mornings
when you wake to charred and smoldering grass
from a cross burned in your neighborhood
when you see a plantation for the first time
and you are not awed by its beauty
but haunted by the slave cabins not included on public tours
when you learn to navigate the historical land mines
when your steps become fluid dance moves in the margins
and your tongue follows with fluent code switch and *switchbacks*
criks, hollers and *down yonders*
when you do not know what the word *kin* means
but when you've been here long enough
you feel how blood circles back

when you truly understand Dorothy's decree as double-edged
There's no place like home There's no place like home

Learning How to Run

for my big brother, Will

Before teaching me to run, you taught me how to listen.
Remember when I didn't want to buy track shoes for tryouts

and I just wanted to run in my old Chuck Taylors?
I asked you "What if I ain't not any good?"

You said, "Trust me." I did.
We went to Sam Wyche's:

bought pearl-white Pumas,
You taught me how to tighten my cleats.

How to walk in like I owned the place
even when we didn't have what Mama said,

a bucket to piss in or a window to throw it out of.
You taught me how to be humble.

How to pitch my weight forward.
How to anticipate the gun.

How to get on my mark: Ready. Set. Go!
How to come out of the blocks low and early.

How to stay in my own lane.
How to fall, but how to get back up.

How to ignore haters,
but definitely talk trash if needed.

So, when some white runners on Southside's
track team called me a *nigger*

you had already taught me this pocket-ready reply.
I'm not a nigger. I'm a negro. When I become a nigger, I'll let you know.

You taught me how to stay focused on the finish line.
How to be propelled by the wind. How to kick at the end.

How to respect what God gave me:
fast twitch muscles with a need for speed.

How to race only against the clock.
How to win.

How to lose and not think my life was over
because tomorrow there's another race.

How to know track is a sport,
but also, a philosophy.

How to *run and not get weary*.
How to put one foot before the other.

How to lean into life: Headfirst.

Boy

I say, boy, pay attention when I'm talkin' to ya, boy.
Foghorn Leghorn

He's pock marked, and bullet ridden.
Learns to dance, duck and dodge

with his head raised or lowered.
He knew either way: they coming for you.

Boy be another way to pin you into place.
Grind metal into precious flesh,

a weighted word aimed and hurled,
meant to maim—slow kill preferably.

At the Poinsett Hotel
he's back-bent busboy busy

clearing tables and washing dishes
trying everything he knows

to grow full height into becoming a man.
His change so short he figures he can't get there from here.

One day he knows, if one more person calls me boy, *I'll kill em.*
Instead of punching the clock the next day,

he finds the Air Force recruitment office.
Signs his whole legal name: Johnny Clifton Redmond,

exchanges apron for fatigues.
Swaps battlefields.

Hang Man (Woman)

As kids, what did we know?
We drew the noose.
We thought it just a guessing game,
but Mama's mouth as scissors
told us otherwise.

Later, I learned what she could not say.
I felt how trees leaned
against our favor.
History's slant.
We were not meant
to be written in but hung.

Now, I carry
the brunt and burden
of all the names spilled,
that I cannot spell
into each and every blank.

Racism Squared

Square dances and town squares
fill me with an inarticulate fire.

How I burned when forced to dance
a folk dance not of my folk.

Even at fifteen, I knew dance
was every shape but square.

My friends and I dressed in all black
preferred our routine to Heat Wave's *Boogie Nights*.

We circled the floor with heads and hips,
even our backs curved to the beat

of bass and drum. Unbeknownst to us
we shimmied in the footsteps of our ancestors.

In gym class, for a grade we were forced
to heed the call, *swing your partner,*

and I was swung into the center
of every southern town I've ever entered,

where the phantom auction block sits,
where the caller barks: *Bidder Bidder Bidder*   *Sold!*

I flinch when fireworks explode.
I can't celebrate or abide parades

papered red, white and blue or Irish green.
People drunk stumble to bad beer

and music that twangs. There were times
when we were dismembered on these streets.

I flash back to whip crack and snap of branches,
to another black man or a black woman

hanging half-mast on trees: while white people feast,
overhead my people swing.

Say Carolina

for my Palmetto State, after Rita Dove

Nothin finer than a tea-drunk gurl
raised on peaches, sugah, honey chile & y'all
Nothin finer than her palmetto & crescent moonshine
pinched and dangling on each ear
Nothin finer than her sass
her sweet potato thick waist
spreading from the low country to the upstate
Bible belt cinched and clinched
sportin 46 patches that work
a rice, cotton & tobacco shimmy
from sunup to sundown
Carolina's hot, but cotton's supposed to let you breathe
but under her honeysuckle & yellow jessamine print skirt
all you feel is the burn of 9,000 ebony fires
& Denmark Vesey leading the charge
whispering in quilt-stitch code
for a stolen people to rise up
sharpen their dreams and fly
Carolina's a gumbo sweet grass grace
mixed with old money
Look down her cobblestone roads
laced with Spanish moss,
you feel the worlds between the worlds
rainbow row colors blending

with auction block songs
Part the veils but don't get too close to her port waters
even if you know how to swim cause
Carolina's deep she's a complicated lady
Look beyond the magnolias and mint juleps
she's all plantation upfront & middle passage baggage behind
She's had a hard time carrying the weight
but Carolina don't care cause she the bomb
all muskets & cannons when she lifts her skirt
Shoot, Carolina will blow your mind
with the twisted & strange fruit
she both bears & wears
Say it again, *Carolina don't care*
She done acquired the taste
You can tell how she walks and talks
she likes how it hangs

Proof of Purchase

Do not fail to get a receipt or put your purchases in a sack
or I'll beat your butt when you come back. Don't make me tell you again.

Don't give white folks reason to accuse you or an excuse to attack.
I've seen us hung for less than that again and again.

If you go out there and get killed, I'll bring you back,
raise you from the dead and I'll kill you all over again.

Mama ain't doing nothing but showing us tough love. True fact.
Drills *Stay alive* in our ears again and again. Hear echo: Again.

Mama didn't raise no fools. Teaches us to watch our backs.
Fight racist barbs and acts thrown in our faces again and again.

When I was married, my husband came home with no bag or
receipt. I cracked.
He's white. I forgot the same rules don't apply for him. I'm
triggered again.

We live in two Americas armed with a double-conscious vision
living while black,
a world where we have to justify our existence again. Repeat again.

Our country was built on black and brown backs.
Still they try to sell us slogans like Make America Great Again.

Since the beginning of this country, we have been suspected and tracked.
Glenis, you understand how history plays hate on repeat. Amnesia ricochets again.

American Tragedy

after William H. Johnson's Sowing I

Almost bucolic pastoral.
Every which way I look,
I see signatures of home home.
Work-weary hats sit on their heads
like radiating planets, the overalls stiff
with a work ethic, the figures not childlike,
but plain folk who could be my Great Aunt Carrie
and my Great Uncle Willie or any other kinfolk. It's the jut of jaw,
the deliberate thrust of seed crop into the earth.
It's the tending to the urgency of needing to survive.
All these tells makes me say: This Us. This We.

Earthbound constellations, impartial histories of Home. Home.
The flare of flesh and knuckle—the no-nonsense self-sufficiency.
In every fiber equipped with an almanac wisdom.
They take up both land and row.
Their many legs, arms, and feet
that inhabit the land suggest work takes every limb.
They are drawn into this contract with lackluster eyes.
What's worse? Hardly a trace of lips.
No teeth. Workhands, but nobody listens to what their mouths say.

Our contribution to this country, the blues,
the truest American art form. Our story (ies) always dipped in blue—

more fractured than lineage.
This is home home too—a broken, beautiful people
given no other way than to see the crop through and through.
Every line meant to press us into a place, no answers
just rows upon rows of work.

Genealogy is always at my foreground,
I always take in what's round: crescent moon, gourd bag, work-
weary eyes,
an impartial telling of South Carolina's diseased history.
Our hunger begs for teeth, lip and bite.

Praise the artist who paints our story,
no matter how broken it is—
at least there's a record by a reliable narrator.
The one I trust is the one who stays.
The one I trust is the one who leaves.
I trust perception armed with a healthy distance.
This painting becomes a rectification.
There's room for how deep the plot truly is.
The land speaks of what is never said.
This void is home home too.
The master painter paints a path out of the frame,
full circles seen and unseen.

I step daily on a double-conscious walk
adorned in colors that I love, orange and yellow,
but the task at hand is how to remain unapologetically black
in a world that insists on taking our story.
Harvest comes in so many forms.
I hang on to what he's captured,
because I come and go too.
This is our migration story—
The leaving and the staying are both true.
Our musician father who left the South
because of his mouth, his straightforward gaze,
and his inability to live under any white person's foot.
This is home home too.
Also, a way to stay alive.
His fleeing preferable
to being strung up a tree.
Leaving is one way to stay,
a form of love of how you hold the land
and how the land holds you
even if you never return,
even if inside you
the land always burns.

Flashback

Walking to the Promise Land

One step can hold the fuel for a whole journey.
You will not find this story in history books.
Like most of the facts about our people from the 1800s,
historians hardly took note, much less fastened our doings
to paper with pen. Our stories must be snatched
from bits and pieces passed down from mouth to mouth.
I have to feel what's held in the land.

While living in the mountains, the ancestors beckoned me,
asked me to go to the Kingdom and put chest to ground. Listen.
Since I've been carrying what they've asked me to hold:
stories of a newly freed man
led by a band of ex-slaves walking from Mississippi
to the border of South and North Carolina.

William's light hue tied him to his master's bloodline.
His father instead of denying him,
saw fit to put letters and figures in his son's head
and coins in his pocket.
Maybe he handed him a map.
Maybe this was his way to put distance
between him and his dark error.
William Jr. contained his own spark, though.
Could make the bible speak.

Drew one hundred and fifty to walk with him
on a five-hundred-and-fifty-mile trek.
I am sure his vision spurred them on
with tales about the river circling a hill.
I bet they could feel their shackles release
and see freedom around the bend—
as they pressed their weary soles one tired foot after another.
I can see them resting alongside the Enoree and trudging up
Callahan Mountain and Winding Stair.

I can feel their faith, knowing they would get there,
a place with a plot to plow linking them shoulder to shoulder
and good intention to will. Their numbers grew.
I can see them with their sweat-laden backs bent.
I can see what woke them every morning,
their own hands and feet touching what they sewed,
their limbs spread wide in their compound
teasing and parsing what grew from walk and work,
as ex-slaves they dared to dream up a space,
dubbed Kingdom of Happy Land.

Cymbee: An Afro Carolinian Mermaid Tale

(1)

Time before, when we were not severed
from bucolic lands rich with awe/hope
one would welcome the burnt orange skies.
Us on the green land, the land
in us. We, part of the Earth—
fierce with the bright light of kinship:
goat, trees, rolling hills and blessed water.

(2)

Birds fly up in the blue high—
track their wing path to before/now,
thrum beating with wonder of the earth.
The river kinks and wanders and meanders.
The herder corrals the beasts to keep.
We come to the water to drink
and we find the spirit of life.

(3)

We know clean water is big medicine.
Water is life. Without water, we know:

First the body withers. Then: spirit dies.
Neither of these are ways to go.
What we know we will always know:
The water that fills us tells us
to follow the way of Simbi. Seek.

(4)

The white men do not believe us.
Say we're what is beneath their feet.
Yet, they wrangle us from our villages.
Their bible says they must rescue us
full of our blue-black savage witchery.
They think we're evil, spin wicked folktales.
Though they pillage the earth for coins.

(5)

Strike of machete. Clash. Boom of gun.
We. Run. Trampled by feet and ghosts.
With deals and a plan. Terror wins.
Loaded on big ships we've never seen.
Over the Atlantic Simbi follows her ward.

Hovers overhead and around the dark hull.
The wind is both her whisper and howl.

(6)

Fervent long prayers sung in manifold tongues.
Whips and lashes we wail loud. Louder.
Our cries, the only thing we possess.
We let our strong chants overtake us—
Sometimes we sound like a blessed choir;
clashing notes sometimes meet in powerful harmony.
We know Simbi will never forsake us.

(7)

We soon fear what we should not.
Water. Men. Ships. Ocean. Love. Life. Ourselves.
Stripped from what we always have known.
Cycles. Seasons. Spirals. Drought. Gift. Simbi. Water.
Where have we failed? In trust? Dust.
Doubt. Loss. Blood. Chains. Stolen. Lost. Torn.
We'll never be what we once were.

(8)

We're now shadows of our better selves.
We are severed people. Enslaved. Not slaves.
We do not know our station yet,
chains. Shackles. Manacles. Clang. Clang and lock
at our wrists and at our ankles.
Bodies side by side we're rubbed raw.
At our open wounds they throw salt.

(9)

On weakened legs they make us dance.
This long nightmare we keep on reliving.
We remember when we danced for Simbi,
offered up our soul to please her.
On steel leashes we jerk and dangle.
Die inside in the face of evil.
When we trance dance we must remember.

(10)

The West says, Mermaid, but she's more.
Simbi sits in the pantheon of Spirits.

She dwells in oceanic blue-black depths.
Water. Born. Fed. Water. Wise. Water. Wielder.
Whirl. Warrior. Wailing. Waves fierce long arms.
At each end fist: fight or hover.
Her reach is either house or jail.

(11)

Simbi there. Cymbee here. Her name: moot.
People of the Congo know her well.
Simbi's spirit must be honored and fed
with each drink, food, dance and treasure.
Without ceasing, she finds reasons to mother.
Wraps her long arms around her people
on either side of the deep Atlantic.

(12)

Come rain. Come flood. Come torrent. Come.
World's balance is off when Simbi's caught.
Until Simbi free we don't know work.
Sit. Sleep. Rest. Pray. Eat. Think. Dream.
We got plenty of sense. Know where

our beautiful blessings come from. Sea. Deep.
Knee-bent we sing for full-body release.

(13)

We are blooming stars—seeds captured. We rise.
We are black water bodies southern beached.
Snatched and tied to land by hands.
We told, but full of telling. Story-filled.
Beware of the lowly ones who overcome.
The one that hits soon forgets. The
one that takes the hit never forgets.

(14)

Know there are two kinds of people.
Those who have Cymbee, those who don't.
With Cymbee. We, ocean-filled vessels seeking more.
We are the song of the sea.
We are that which can't be named.
We are blue, green, gray, black cosmos.
We leap on dry land. Find water.

(15)

In our tears, sweat and stolen kisses,
we keep our history wet with memory.
Every act we make. River and pond:
places of true hallowed ground for Simbi.
We find ways to worship and swim.
We, the blackest blue beauty. Carolina bred.
Ancient lights. Stolen, but belong to Africa.

An Exercise in Restraint,
a Letter to Ann Cunningham

Dear Mrs. Ann Cunningham:

I came across your home, The Rosemont Plantation, in my
research on South Carolina history. I immediately called my Mama
to let her know what I had found, as she grew up in the same town
of Waterloo. When I told her the name of the estate, she said,
"Cunningham." "Yes," I said, "that's the name of the family that
owned the estate." Mom replied, "That's also Grandma's surname."
Rachel Cunningham. For the past ten years, I have prodded Mama
to tell me Rachel's last name, but she could not remember it, until I
mentioned the plantation, then she unearthed it.

Mrs. Cunningham, there's no way for me to bring this up gently;
I believe that your family owned mine. The truth that no black or
white person wants to hear or bear, but here I am offering it up, my
face not turned away from this force. But I must tell you though
I appear bold, I am as broken as my family line. In me and in us,
there's a deep well that needs to be filled. The words *owned and owe*
though they are only two letters from being the same, are worlds
apart in their meaning, as are the two of us.

Mrs. Cunningham, I am writing to you because I know that
you hold your family dear, as I read of the work you have done
to revitalize your family estate. I also understand that you ran
a similar campaign for Mt. Vernon. As a dutiful daughter, I am
doing the same for my family, though not with a home, but with

my lineage. I would like to trace and make it as whole as possible. I would like to acknowledge and honor my ancestors who came before me and with my words, I plan to leave my ancestors standing, intact, and with the dignity every person wants and deserves.

Mrs. Cunningham, I would appreciate your prompt response to this letter. Though almost two centuries separate us, I have nowhere else to turn, just you, replying from beyond time. I would most appreciate any information regarding my ancestors: ledgers, proof of purchase, anecdotes or especially keepsakes, that remain in your possession, as they would be both valued and honored in my family.

I would also be pleased to learn Rachel's parents' names and to learn how they spent their days. I do not consider this too much to ask, as my freedom is intricately woven into theirs. I am waiting for their feathers to add to my wings.

Sincerely,

Glenis Redmond

Freedom Spells 1

for Harriet Tubman

Deep brown. Crooked switch of a gal. Born under a serious bright but sickly star. Measle-pocked. Faints a lot. Me, a sight: Hair never seen a comb. When I feel my head or catch my likeness in a lake, it be *standing up around my head like a bushel basket.* Gal mostly still baby, but no slave stay a child for long.

My Mama do her best wid wat she had to make me well again: victuals and a bit of de bible she done learn. She fed me both. I growed in and out of de fever and whatever else ailing.

Owned by Massa Cook. His face scrunched like a rabid dog all de time. When I still weak, he made me wade in de water to fetch muskrats. Almost drownded. He say, "You ain't worth six pence" or yell, "Ise sell you down river." I close my eyes and shut my ears. That my way of spitting on dat. Dis when I become I, not she, become like dat Oak standing in de yard firm in her roots. What hold her steady, help me hold my ground.

Dey call me to de house tho. I hate every wall. I call it cage in my mind, so you know what dat make me. Can't stand mistress' reach either. Seem like her eyes be every which way at once. Her command too. She tell me when to take in air and when to let it out. Everything at my fingers, but none of it mine.

I stole a little taste a sugah once. One lump, cause I ain't never had nothin sweet on my tongue. Lashed for dat, but I padded myself wid as much cloth as I could find, so when she whup me, I commence to hollering. Caterwauling, but ise do wat I gots to do. I laughs on de inside. Just something between me and my maker. Ise five feet even and full of everythang de Lawd put in me. Stubborn. My giddy up don't go unless I say so.

Field over house any day. I knows my way around every inch of work: Hoist flour bags. Break flax. Pick cotton wid my eyes close. My weight be slight, but my muscle be strong. Wid de Almighty on my side, who stand again me? In de field. I feel de strength in my arms and legs. Feel what my Mama poured into me: de soil under my feets and my lungs full of clean air. I earned more dan I ever owed. I put dem coins away til dey collect. I buys not a pretty dress, but two steers. When riding, I hold de reins and I sip de air as I need.

Spells for Zero Captures

Conduct like I ain't tryin to die. Leave when de moon new. Sky
dark. Listen to what on my inside, cause it don't lie. When my chest
flutters, I knows danger lurks. Change course. "Know I can't die
but once." But, ain't tryin to do dat just yet. Don't speak on nothin.
No peacocking. Proud talk get you dead. No need for *I did dis and I
did dat*. Blend into tree trunk. Travel in winter. Buy time. Saturday
night rewards for runaways not in papers till Monday morn. Got
a whole day before dey spect we gone. Read people and de land
like white people read books. When I have a spell, shout not. Don't
fight deep sleep. Go into de body quake. Vision and dreams be
how God directs my path. Follow de map dat my inside knows. Let
God talk. No open field in daylight. Know de codes like I know de
woods. Light in window. No trails. Cover footsteps. Don't give into
thoughts of coon dogs and guns. Quiet steps. Silence. Give babies
de root. Paregoric. My Grandma Modesty came over on de boat
from Africa. She knew de earth holds medicine. Listen to de old
ways. Don't tarry. Make friends of weary and tired. Dey don't leave
no how. "You'll be free or die." Don't turn back. Trust de Quakers,
but carry a gun loaded anyhow. Curse slavers. "Never wound a
snake; kill it." "God's time Emancipation is always near." He set de
North Star in de heavens." He gave me de strength in my limbs to
follow where his light leads.

Every One of My Names

for Harriet Tubman

Every one of my names I earned.
cept de first: Araminta Ross
given to me at birth.
Didn't take too much to it.
Cause it sounds like a flower standing in a field.
Araminta. Araminta. Got God's covering.
I keep de prayer and music from it.
For short dey say *Minty*.
I like how dat sing. Got more of my sting.
I stood up to massa no matter who was wronged,
but he head-butted me into dreams and visions.

Took Tubman from my man.
My husband left me, cause I wouldn't stay put
to his need and de cabin.
One of de times I came back
freeing peoples he in de arms of another woman.
He axed me in de middle of my heart wit dat.
Lawd knows I loved him.
Lawd knows he loved me too,
but I was meant for more.
I belong to de many.

Dey calls me Harriet.
I took Harriet from my Mama.
Her love circle around me
like my wrap around my head,
like my shawl hugs my shoulders.
Dey call me brave, cause I wrap
my long arms around my peoples.

Dis how I stand: rooted and ready for battle.
Dis is how I love—fitted for fight.
My face is not fixed on pleasing—
what good is a smile in war?
I busy in battle.

Called me Conductor too cause I head dis foot train
with hounds at my bloody feet.
I runs and I runs.
I told Fredrick Douglass once
I ain't never lost a passenger.
I know which way is North with my ear to God's mouth.

General too dey call me, cause I at de head,
where no woman supposed to be,
but I outsmart every slaver's hunt.

Fear for what? Once I break chains,
I release de minds on being a slave next.
No matter what dey call me—
I'm on a mission.
If dey even thinkin about turnin back,
I point pistol to head.
Say, *A dead negro tells no tale.*
Dis be de way my spirit rise up.
My fire be both a curse and a blessin.
Dis fire burns—never snuffed out.

Dey call me Moses—cause mah people mus go free.
Dey whisper me spy too, when dey speak of me
cause I got my hand in so many plots.

Dey give me names
so many names
most of dem mannish—
but by God's grace I go
wid a long skirt
with these able hands
to answer every call
—all woman.

More Than What My Mistress Makes

There seemed no one capable of enduring the oppression of the
house but her.
Harriet E. Wilson

Born free I was still dragged
by my spirit from sunup to sundown,
a daughter of a hooper of barrels,
a daughter of a washerwoman.

My knuckle's blood, my Mama's
callused legacy. My curved spine,
my papa's inheritance. My dark skin,
hung on me like a shadow.

With it I face the heat of hate. I lived my childhood
roof squashed and singed by my mistress's breath
housebound pressed, lash-tied to obedience.
Dragged by my spirit from sunup to sundown.

My neck squirms to somebody else's clock.
I swing to this borrowed cadence.
My dance is drag, shuffle, and kick ball chain.
I dangle to the strain of a short leash,

a tightened noose, with a tag, *Our Nig*.
This is how I am called less than the family dog.

Under my tongue there is prayer.
Under my tongue there is civility,

but no one would ever know,
because my mouth is tamed,
my dreams squelched, but I am more
than what my mistress makes of me.

I am fashioned by a force greater
than her will, stronger than her rawhide slash,
boot tip, and poison whipping of words.
My mistress always makes a cruel point,

but my rage is the sharpest blade
in this house, a keen tip fashioned
by her edge. I am destined to slice strife.
In my chest a hurricane stirs my heart,

the whoosh sounds like a familiar friend.
Harriet my name, an elixir I drink
when pressed between earth and sky.
From this deep well I fueled by more.

More than what my mistress makes of me.
I am stirred—not by *Our Nig*,
but *Harriet*, a tested fire,
forged by my own making.

House: Another Kind of Field

for Harriet Jacobs

This house big, but the way I am held by his hands, I am a tight
fist. I tiptoe and flinch around every corner. Over my shoulder is
where my eyes live. This body I carry, not mine. My chest heaves
all day. High yellow. Light bright. Almost white. Whatever color I
am called—his gaze burns me, so does his hands. I am kept closer
than his wife. He leaves me nothing but bruised blue. I, house
nigger—not one step up from, but another kind of down. House,
be another way to say: field. He makes me feel like the dirt he walks
on. Upturned and plowed. His teeth metal rakes across my skin.
His mouth and his hands don't do nothing but take: rip, tear and
thrust. I bleed and breed. Chains seen or unseen, my feet, still
shackled. This is not the life the Almighty meant for me, but no
choice is what I got. The only place I run far is in my mind. I keep
my lips shut, but every scream I don't shout is loud within me.
Every scream adds up to flee. My feet become my mind. They carry
me to where Grandma stay. She free. How I'd like to just lie down
in her arms and rest for always, but ain't no rest for a hunted slave.
Light bright. Almost white. Whatever color I am called—his gaze
finds me. This body I carry, not my own. My chest heaves all day.
Grandma attics me away. When I walk through her upstairs door, I
don't know if I will ever be free. This attic feels like a pine box. My
feet can't wander many feet yonder, but a few steps. My hands, my
arms, my legs God gifted me can't stretch. I am a bent star dwelling
in shuttered light. So small my world seems. Low roof and tight

walls make like my grave. This attic could be a pine box closing, but in my chest, I feel an opening. Above his reach, the less I feel like a kept thing. This room dark most days, but I see myself clear. I dance a dance in this place of tight walls and roof to break his white grasp. I wiggle. I weave. I work—not seven days, seven weeks, seven months but seven years of bearing heat and cold. Where a rat's bite—the only touch I know. I am bent by this stay, but I fix my mind for when that door opens. I am ready to fling myself wide and take up any space in this world. Star-spread and wide.

Dreams Speak: My Father's Words

for Harriet E. Wilson

I had to coax my heart open to see
what my bones already knew. Follow

how the blood road travels back
to understand—how the tree root shoots

from solid ground. If I stand still
long enough, I can feel how the earth turns

by my father's dark hand. How he lifts
the veil, so I can stare into the worlds

between the worlds. The branched bottles
hold his clear voice as he dream speaks

in my ear. Shows me how destiny's wheel turns.
How trouble will hound me most of my days.

How grief will rob me of my son,
my beloved held at my breast.

How work will beat my body down.
How trouble will stand next to me like kin.

Bedridden, I will beg to die,
but he chants, fair daughter, rise.

You will rise and follow the leaves.
The call of my dream voice will guide you

to trace your palms. Close your eyes.
Feel the pulse. See how the future connects

to your strong lifeline. Your legacy
will be blown on bottles, etched in books.

Gifts held by others. You will be known as:
The Earnest Eloquent Clairvoyant.

On this dirt path paved, you will conjure
what the world hands you. Navigate the heart.

Your palms smooth jagged rocks into fortune.
Divine daughter dance between those worlds.

Curtains drawn open. Peer. Gain inner sight.
See how at the core all turns and turns.

Extracting Light or How to Get Here from There
for solar eclipse, August 21, 2017

I don't know much about history
  Sam Cook

or astrology or nothing really about anything
of one celestial body blocking the light of another
but I do understand the power of a shadow's eclipse
how I have stumbled from the loss of light in a room
The room is history
The stubbed toe: my ignorance
There is no me without the brightest light
in my constellation, Mama
I marvel at how I have traveled this far
thinking I've gained many miles
being the first in my family proper
to gain a college degree masters even,
but I ain't traveled nowhere
till I look back and catch the gold
Mama spins and weaves
I am unearthing threads and knitting light
to help me see through this dark night
With no moon glow or sunlight it is hard
to see myself clear
but always it dawns on me
to form a question

Take the quest
Sometimes I am just slow
but I get there   here:
Mama are you the first person in the family
to graduate from high school?
I am standing in her garage
in Canterbury my childhood home
The poet-to-poet connection is not lost on me
On First Day Street she stares
brown eyes ringed blue like Saturn
Yes she says your dad and I
graduated in the last class
from Fountain Inn Negro High School
To get there from here
follow me down a back road
where every memory clings
like red clay dust
You will need these items for sight:
A black cast iron cauldron
5 buckets water hauled from the well
1 large stick
Lye soap
Bluing
Clothes pins

Clothesline
Argo starch
Iron
Scrub board
Dirty laundry
Firewood
A mother's will
A daughter's hope

One day starts with a spark in a daughter's eye
she asks for a high school ring
she does not get a po' mouth parent's quip
of *Money don't grow on trees*
or, *This ain't no gimme South Carolina*
She's met with her mother's mind and hands
set on giving what she asked for
what she herself never had—
not just a ring, but a way out of Waterloo
even though she'd been branded
by *You can't get there from here.*
Black woman with a third-grade education
sent her daughter to live
with her Aunt Carrie and Uncle Willie in Greenville County
Laurens had no schools for *coloreds*

The coins she collected for taking in washing
wasn't the only sense she had
She had triple and quadruple loads
Buckets of water toted
She knew how to put match to dry kindling and her will
bring well water to a strong boil
This takes a while
She had time and made the best of it
You know what they say about a watched pot
She put eye and knuckle to scrub board
to already presoaked stained garments
Rumor was: she washed the whitest whites for the whites
Hard work but she did not give up
unlike the blood piss and red clay
under her work weary wrinkled hands
No one knew how she chanted over each garment.
Yea though I walk through the valley of the shadow
of death I will fear no evil
Whatever it took to ease the mind
while spine curved over the soiled:
crease of collar crotch of panties baby diapers
Cigarette always hung from the crook of her mouth
lip pressed around a tan butt while she released smoke
Sometimes she muttered a blessing or a curse

say *Shit* drawn out long and slow
as if she were trying to lift the stank
First by word then by hand
You didn't hear it told from me
or she just sang What a friend we have in Jesus
Whether curse or prayer each garment
wrenched like a chicken neck
Draw the water out to make faster work
Pin clothes on the line to meet sun and wind
Clean and dry clothes ain't the end
but another beginning
Heat iron on stove Sprinkle starch
to tamp down hunger
Munch on some too
Press every white thang flat like new money
Fold into brown paper parcels
Hand to daughter to collect 25¢ pieces
Do this over and over until enough
Forget pomp and circumstance
Mama places high school ring
on daughter's finger
Breaks curses
Beats back blues
indigo and midnight

Daughter carries the light
never forgets to shine
what's passed down the line.

A Dollar a Day

The first in her line of women to hire a maid
sixty years later, she's still a knotted rope.
"She cleaned our house three days a week,
to help the economy, a military mandate."
Mama wanted to stand elbow to elbow with her.
Clean the way she was taught: Wipe spills
and messes. Scrub pots. Sweep a room clean.
Mama was raised on, *If you don't have something to do,*
I'll find you something to do.
Her name was Fatima, named for one of the women in the Koran
as the daughter of Muhammed,
means *captivating daughter.*
Fatima cleaned the whole house with her baby
strapped on her back.
Took all the shoes out of the closets daily.
Mama remembers the dust of the desert in Morocco.
Shakes her head, *it covered everything.*
Looks on as Fatima fishes
the tinfoil out of the trash.
Watches her press the foil flat
to take leftovers home to her family of five.
How did she feel about Mama's
fried chicken and macaroni and cheese?
Mama's name: Jeanette. Means *The Lord is gracious.*

I muse about these two women
countries and religions between them
bonded as sisters by make-do ways.

Flight

Ode to What's Owed a Stitch at a Time

The foot-pedaled Singer sewing machine
sits still in Mama's dining room
—sings a song older than anyone in the house
—not the electric tune, but the tick-tock music of a clock.

I muse on how you pulsed when fed fabric by Grandma's
mahogany know-how hands—making whatever she imagined:
calico curtains, flour-sack dresses, castoffs stitched together to
make quilts.

Now, you stand for decoration not duty draped in doilies,
but if I lean in, I can make out a steady pluck—
feel the push and pull of patching and piecing
—sounds like a holy choir,
a homespun quilt of all the women who begat:
Angelina begat Hanna
Hanna begat Rachel
Rachel begat Katie
Katie begat Jannie, Jeanette and Dorothy
Janie begat Lucille, Queen and Lisa
Dorothy begat Denise
Jeanette begat Velinda and Glenis
Velinda begat Onisha and Donna

Glenis begat Celeste and Amber
Celeste begat Paisley.

We all began by hand—
mother teaching daughter
how to pierce the eye of the needle.
Spear the tip with spit.
Then, how to knot the thread
with thumb and index finger. Roll.

You are silent, but your plodding is in my blood.
Though I never worked your craft,
I pick up the ink pen.
Make quilts from tattered memories.
Now, I stand in front of people speaking poetry,
clad in a dress sewn by all my mothers.
Swathed in patches of yam, indigo, and cotton
stretched from Cameroon to the Carolinas,
tightened with stiches held fast from humble gatherings.

When Mama Dreams of Fish or
Black Folk Superstitions

after Elizabeth Acevedo

Mama in one breath recites:

*Yea though I walk through the valley
and shadow of death, I will fear no evil.*

In next breath, *Don't open that umbrella in my house,
it's bad luck. Don't court trouble.*

When she dreams of fish, upon waking
immediately asks, *Who's pregnant?*

*Itch in the right palm foretells
money's coming.* On New Year's Day,

she cooks collards for an abundance of dollars
and black-eyed peas for plentiful change.

Mama never places her purse on the floor,
so she won't go broke,

but with wave of hand and tsk of tongue says,
I don't believe in that foolishness.

What I hear her say is, *Don't do as I do, but do as I say do,*
as she calls on Jesus, while simultaneously

burns her hair retrieved from her brush,
so the strands can't be gathered for root work.

If a bird pecks on your window or a picture
falls off the wall, death is near.

If a spider drops before you on its web,
A stranger's coming to visit.

Gain a man's heart through his stomach,
to keep him put, bury his drawers in the front yard.

She shoos me away when I have broom in hand.
Don't sweep my feet, I might want to marry again.

Reading crows: *One for trouble,*
two to receive a letter and three for joy,

and a gray-headed child is to be cherished,
for that child will be both wise and rich.

When walking never split a pole with a person
you love, or the relationship will be severed.

Don't tell your wishes or wants to anyone,
or they will be snatched on the wind.

In hushed whispers she always warns,
Every shut eye ain't sleep and every goodbye ain't gone.

As a child, I never really knew what Mama meant,
but I've learned as my mother's daughter

to see between her words and sense
the world with my eyes closed.

The Wind in My Name

What my Mama and daddy handed down
on the day before King's "I Have a Dream" speech—
Glenis Gale Redmond is grounded—is what's real.
I don't need no stage name. No hip-hop moniker.

My parents knew their baby girl born in the 60s
needed to be fit with two black fists.
Irony aside of the Celtic twist of the slave holder's grip.
I like the tight fit of my two Welsh names: Glenis Gale.
Valley on one hand and wind on the other.
Ancestral forces at my back while I face the Shadow of Death:

The decade of killing into which I was born.
King on the balcony of the Lorraine,
Evers in Mississippi in his own driveway.
The bullets that struck Malcolm seven times
on 166th and Broadway and Mama's brother, Uncle Pete,
killed by his so-called doctor, "Boy take these pills.
Ain't nothin wrong with you but lazy."
Only for him to die the next day
on his living room couch at age twenty-four.

There's real hurt in this hurricane.
So, there's no pretense, just urgency

and I need every fiber in my fast-twitch muscle
as I blow past pain, as I run like the wind in my name.
They don't like it when we run.
Made laws against our legs poised in the arc of freedom.

String me up by my given name, they try to call me
out of *nigger, bitch, wench, gal and ho.*
The noose they want me to work and twerk to.
Before I dance that swing and dangle.
But I got blood memory running
like a fever in my name.
So, I jerk possess with spirits unrest
to the cunning in Cunningham,
slave holders that gave my great-grandma her last name.
Silencing the shackle of those who never rebelled,
but left the plot in me stirring with these songs of freedom.

They say, *It's wind*
but I believe it is *fire* in my belly.
I feel my great-grandma rising
in my name off the Rosemont Plantation
in Waterloo, South Carolina.

This ain't no play play, but for real.
I try to keep it real even at age 9.
Mama says, *stop acting so mannish.*
But you know legs crossed, hair restrained
like a dog on a chain ain't headed nowhere.
And lower your voice because loud ain't lovely,
but quiet is not in my nature.
If you expected it to be,
probably shouldn't have named me after the jet
that broke the sound barrier, Glamorous Glennis.
Destiny and fate dictate I break laws of gravity.
The black ink turned into wings
that morph into the music in the spiritual.
The teeth
                    the tongue
                                    the lungs

                                                    the asthmatic breath
all in this name.
I got ground holding me down, geography
in my name. Cherokee mountains.
I said I got red in this name.
The West Coast of Africa: Cameroon and Nigeria.
Leaf and Bone,

the struggle of the slave port.
Auction block to sweetgrass in my name.

I got fire.
I got ammunition in this name.
I feel like our female Moses
running under and over ground.
In my name holding pens and paper
to people's hands and hearts
saying, *Write your way out.*

I got griots of Africa,
bards of Wales,
tellers of Indian tales.

I, Glenis up everything
personal and collective history.
Wind is a serious force not to be toyed with.
No cubic zirconia gleam, no pretend in me.
No persona wanna be—just my grandma saying,
All you gotta do is stay black and die
and that's what she did after 109 years.
I write what she couldn't in my name.
Live and give breath in my name.

I'm a force that breathes life into voice.
Take what my Mama and daddy gave me.
Grounded and rooted in what's real,
I claim all this in my name.

Caged Bird Sings Because

honoring Maya Angelou

Singing be better
than weeping
ask Billie and Nina

Sings cause she's born bound
belts blues
through shut doors
with throat open wide
sings raw truth

Sings cause sky calls
and she's more wild than cage
so she beat wings
against bars finds music
in pen upon paper upon heart

She sings cause her dark skin mirrors night sky
deep down she knows
not everyone loves her back
not everyone loves her black
velvet contrast against moonshine

Knows her full lips and even fuller nose
in this white world be   acquired taste.

She sings cause she can't erase
Dr. Kenneth & Mamie Clark's Doll Experiment 1940s
Proves what everybody knows
White child picks white doll
Black child picks white doll   still

She sings cause
Stamps, Arkansas
and Sumter, South Carolina
holds black girls the same way
dome squashed with low expectations

Caged bird sings
cause broken wing hurt
did not begin with her
been passed down
She comes from a long line
of birds who will not fly

Caged bird sings cause
she needs exit stratagies
Reads Maya Angelou's books
like road maps till she caged no more

Caged bird conducts
her own experiment
instead of dolls
black girl chooses black woman self
takes her likeness off the shelf

Each song she sings,
mantra-like affirmations
recites them over and over again
phenomenal woman phenomenally
sings until she believes
that's me. That's me.

Imagining Frida Kahlo as My Life Coach

1.

Woman. Draw yourself in, but always in layers.

Note: Jewels tones of ruby and azure,

contrast brilliantly against brown hues.

The world will tell you how the self-portrait

and the first person "I" do not matter.

My paintings beg to differ.

They thought I was a Surrealist, but I wasn't.

I never painted dreams. I painted my own reality.

Create your crucial cartography.

Go against the shallow grain

in craft and within yourself.

See how I let my eyebrows meet?

Proving beauty does not have to be pruned.

Make your own standards of loveliness.

To honor my long line of mothers on my mother's side,

I cloaked myself in Isthmus of Tehuantepec.

I braided my hair into an updo crown.

Adorned my lobes and chest with jewels of Oaxaca.

Take heed and revere your African/Southern/Cherokee

foremothers.

Wear talismans from each line for direction and protection.

Let them see what you want them to see.

To deflect from my flaws and fractures,

I wrapped myself in Rebozo shawls
and donned Tehuana dresses and long skirts:
Appearances are meant to be deceiving.

2.
Go within.
Slice beyond skin.
Thirty operations could take me nowhere,
but within. *I turned pain into inspiration.*
When that pole pierced my pelvis,
I took my bedridden sentence
as a license to paint. Create at all costs.
Do not cave even though cancer
and fibromyalgia cling to you.
Don't throw the monkeys off your back.
Bid them to sit on your arms and shoulders.
Draw them in.
Do not flinch from what you see within the inner landscape.
Grandmother Death held my hand daily.
I see you sister mystic: How you cavort with death.
Follow the veined territory.
Exhibit your extracted heart.
Be brave wild woman.

3.

Cast out hurt.

I sheared my head in mourning.

My love for him made me falter.

Miscarriages created caverns.

Whatever you do, do not offer your heart

on a silver platter to anyone unless it's even exchange.

Damn, Diego that toad-eye glutton.

He killed me countless times.

Nevertheless, mi amore.

His artist eye could only see me

in parts: pear shaped ass, elongated nape of neck

and the hue of my skin the color of adobe.

He shouts, "Viva la Revolución," for the people,

but could not see the person right in front of him.

With my sister? Predictable philanderer.

Curse him for my love for him—cursed me.

4.

Exorcise.

I blurred every line–especially with sex.

Dressed in men's suits.

Smoked cigars.

Loved women.

Drank tequila straight.

Spread legs wide, when sitting,

to know what it felt like to take up space as a man.

Did not give a damn about who and what I broke, even myself.

Do not do as I did. Do not break yourself more than life breaks you.

5.

Direct gaze into yourself.

See straight through to the other side.

Mythologize.

Put yourself back together the best you can.

With paint. With pen. With purpose.

Even with your chemotherapy-withered-bald-head-self.

Don't flinch. Reinvent.

With one leg gone, I flung the limb.

I adapted the adage, *Why do I need feet when I got wings?*

whenever facing the impossible—

Never say die: Unfurl. Fling. Flare. Fly.

Sketch

for Harriet E. Wilson

Draw the face so we may stare
at the rotten teeth truth.

Give yourself a pristine mouth
to say your piece, through the crude doorway

into a home on history's page
where you're not hemmed in at the margins.

With a determined hand, write the wrong.
Right it! Press your free hand upon parchment.

Spill ink like night clouds
that clot what your soul cannot hold.

Catch what history hurls.
Double your fist in defiance,

unfurl your world into long lines.
Get straight to the point:

Pen every deed. Record the heavy dreams
that woke you each morning.

Press down. The paper can bear your weight.
Make the page speak of back break,

the quill quiver with nothing less than the meat of it.
Whip the naked flesh of the past like you were slashed.

Bleed deep—gash history,
even if it must stand on hobbled legs.

No begging or bowing,
stand in your place.

Ink firm your existence out of the shadows.
Make history one deliberate letter at a time,

not as slave but not fully free either.
Write it the best you can.

Press your free hand upon your heart.
Unbind your mind no matter

how the hand wavers.
This is how perfect penmanship feels,

one liberated turn after the other.
Head the helm. Write your ending.

Right the sky. Burn through fog, mist and muck.
Through your eyes, sketch a new horizon

pulled and drawn by your own hand.

RSVPing to Lucille Clifton

come celebrate
with me that everyday
something has tried to kill me
and has failed.
Lucille Clifton

I got your invitation
and it was right on time.
Up off the couch I rose
from the doctor's prognosis:
You won't die from this, but you'll
sure wish that you would have.
In the clutch of this craw,
I pray for release.

You said, *come celebrate with me.*
I arrived late to the party,
with my poetry shoes on.
I sang loud and off key, full throated,
with no apologies.
With your invitation I take stock
of my black woman passage.
You instructed me to make it up.
I did, follow your lead
between *starshine and clay.*

Every time they try
to break me in Babylon
I summon shango,
shimmy a limbo
with each thrust & jut,
I live.

How I Write

Out of hunger I find myself here
with teeth in stomach
I lean into the ache—
crack my whole self against
kitchen island edge,
so much is born here
in this place where I cook.
My foremothers—
they are all here too
standing right behind me
dressed in the indigo of the cosmos—
no recipe or cookbook in hand
just ten thousand hearts singing.
It's time for you to know too, Glenis.
They pour into me.
With one hand
I let the yolk spill
into the container of the poem.
Turn known and unknown.
Blend with the salt of my tears
and the cayenne of my rage
that I have planned a lifetime around.
They hand me what they have at hand:
Dust from stars, water from rivers

always red clay of the Palmetto
or the West Coast of the Motherland.
In this heat I prepare,
bake, broil, and stew.
Only when they say, "Ready"
do I set the table of page and stage,
serve what I was born to live and give.
Machete with sharpest blade
they hold my heart just so
in my pen they fill
blood and dreams.
In unison they chant, "Now write."

Acknowledgments

Some of these poems first appeared in: 1 A (NPR), 805 Lit + Art, Blue Nib, Crashtest Magazine, EMRYS, Fall Lines, Kakalak, Live Encounters American Poets & Writers, Meridians, New York Times, North Carolina Literary Review, Obsidian: Literature & Arts in the African Diaspora, Orion Magazine, Ripple Effect, Silver Birch Press, storySouth, Tidal Basin Review, and the Weekly Hubris.

Sincere gratitude to my own listening skin. It took me a long time to embrace my highly sensitive nature. Elaine N. Aron's book, The Highly Sensitive Person, enabled me to classify and understand myself. This work helped me locate why I react to people, places, and sensations the way I do. Having this foundational information about HSPs gave me both context and agency to operate in the world.

I am appreciative to Dr. P. Gabrielle Foreman and Dr. Lynnette Overby for true collaboration. Our work together helped me to generate the Harriet poems and the David Drake poem in this book and other David poems being published in our Praise Songs for David Drake collection. My work with these two women has been a labor of historical love. Thank you to Jan Freeman for early edits of this manuscript. Also, thank you to the literary journals that provided and still provide a literary community and home for me, especially during Covid-19. I want to especially thank Orion Magazine, North Carolina Literary Review, and storySouth for championing my work and helping me to move forward as a creative.

I am grateful to all the cities that have embraced me—Greenville, South Carolina; Asheville, North Carolina; Washington, DC; and New Brunswick, New Jersey. People in those places have made space for me to work as a poet and teaching artist. Thank you to Megan Riegel, the CEO at the Peace Center for the Performing Arts, for your support and belief in my poetic outreach mission. Thank you for giving me a space to land as the Poet-in-Residence in my hometown of Greenville. Thank you to Lian Farrer for our work at the State Theatre in New Brunswick, NJ. Our work together helped to inspire some of the poems in this collection. Thank you to the Kennedy Center for the Performing Arts. Thank you especially to Amy Duma and Ellen Westkaemper for finding me on my poet warrior path. You both supported the early stages of my teaching artistry and poetry and you both helped make sure that I became a Kennedy Center Teaching Artist. As a Kennedy Center Teaching Artist, I have been able to provide outreach to school districts and performing arts centers across the country. Thank you to the South Carolina Arts Commission and especially the Executive Director David Platts for friendship and supporting my work. Thank you to Cave Canem. Also, thank you to Julyan Davis for our Cymbee creative partnership during a dire time of my life—going through a stem cell transplant. You have been a great artistic support. I am so thankful for Cymbee. She graced me during this time.

I am grateful to be inspired by all my ancestors, but especially my grandmother Katie Latimore and great-grandmother Rachel Cunningham. Thank you to my Aunt Dot for her spirit and acceptance of my Free-Spirit Ways. Also, much love for my forefathers, Johnny Redmond, Will Rogers, Will Todd and Pete Rogers. I continue to glean from South Carolina, a place that has both molded and shaped me. For those here and now, I am blessed to have my wonderfully creative daughters, Amber Sherer and Celeste Sherer Farmand for their constant love and support. Thank you to all my siblings and our shared history, they are Velinda Simmons, Will Redmond, Errick Redmond, and Jeffery Redmond. I am and will always be eternally grateful to my greatest cheerleader, my Mama, Jeanette Redmond. Her unwavering support has taught me to keep striving and have faith through all things.

A huge thank you to Martha Rhodes for accepting this manuscript and to Sally Ball, Ryan Murphy, Rachel Reeher, and the whole Four Way Books staff. I am pleased to be part of the Four Way Books Family.

Glenis Redmond is an award-winning poet. She has been a literary community leader for almost thirty years. She is a Kennedy Center Teaching Artist and a Cave Canem alum. Glenis has been the mentor poet for the National Student Poets Program since 2014. In the past she prepared these exceptional youth poets to read at the Library of Congress, the Department of Education, and for First Lady Michelle Obama at the White House.

She is a North Carolina Literary Fellowship recipient and helped to create the first Writer-in-Residence position at the Carl Sandburg Home National Historic Site in Flat Rock, North Carolina. Her work has been showcased on NPR and PBS and has been most recently published in *Orion Magazine* and *The New York Times*.

She has three published books and will have three more published in 2022: *The Three Harriets & Others* (chapbook), *The Listening Skin*, and *Praise Songs for Dave the Potter*, art by Jonathan Green and poetry by Glenis Redmond.

In 2020, Glenis received the highest art award in the state of South Carolina: the Governor's Award. She will be inducted into the South Carolina Academy of Authors this spring. She believes poetry is the mouth that speaks when all other mouths are silent.

Publication of this book was made possible by grants and donations. We are also grateful to those individuals who participated in our 2021 Build a Book Program. They are:

Anonymous (16), Maggie Anderson, Susan Kay Anderson, Kristina Andersson, Kate Angus, Kathy Aponick, Sarah Audsley, Jean Ball, Sally Ball, Clayre Benzadón, Greg Blaine, Laurel Blossom, adam bohannon, Betsy Bonner, Lee Briccetti, Joan Bright, Jane Martha Brox, Susan Buttenwieser, Anthony Cappo, Carla and Steven Carlson, Paul and Brandy Carlson, Renee Carlson, Alice Christian, Karen Rhodes Clarke, Mari Coates, Jane Cooper, Ellen Cosgrove, Peter Coyote, Robin Davidson, Kwame Dawes, Michael Anna de Armas, Brian Komei Dempster, Renko and Stuart Dempster, Matthew DeNichilo, Rosalynde Vas Dias, Kent Dixon, Patrick Donnelly, Lynn Emanuel, Blas Falconer, Elliot Figman, Jennifer Franklin, Helen Fremont and Donna Thagard, Gabriel Fried, John Gallaher, Reginald Gibbons, Jason Gifford, Jean and Jay Glassman, Dorothy Tapper Goldman, Sarah Gorham and Jeffrey Skinner, Lauri Grossman, Julia Guez, Sarah Gund, Naomi Guttman and Jonathan Mead, Kimiko Hahn, Mary Stewart Hammond, Beth Harrison, Jeffrey Harrison, Melanie S. Hatter, Tom Healy and Fred Hochberg, K.T. Herr, Karen Hildebrand, Joel Hinman, Deming Holleran, Lillian Howan, Thomas and Autumn Howard, Catherine Hoyser, Elizabeth Jackson, Jessica Jacobs and Nickole Brown, Christopher Johanson, Jen Just, Maeve Kinkead, Alexandra Knox, Lindsay and John Landes, Suzanne Langlois, Laura Lauth, Sydney Lea, David Lee and Jamila Trindle, Rodney Terich Leonard, Jen Levitt, Howard Levy, Owen Lewis, Matthew Lippman, Jennifer Litt, Karen Llagas, Sara London and Dean Albarelli, Clarissa Long, James Longenbach, Cynthia Lowen, Ralph and Mary Ann Lowen, Ricardo Maldonado, Myra Malkin, Jacquelyn Malone, Carrie Mar, Kathleen McCoy, Ellen McCulloch-Lovell, Lupe Mendez, David Miller, Josephine Miller, Nicki Moore, Guna Mundheim, Matthew Murphy and Maura Rockcastle, Michael and Nancy Murphy, Myra Natter, Jay Baron Nicorvo, Ashley Nissler, Kimberly Nunes, Rebecca and

Daniel Okrent, Robert Oldshue and Nina Calabresi, Kathleen Ossip,
Judith Pacht, Cathy McArthur Palermo, Marcia and Chris Pelletiere,
Sam Perkins, Susan Peters and Morgan Driscoll, Patrick Phillips,
Robert Pinsky, Megan Pinto, Connie Post, Kyle Potvin, Grace Prasad,
Kevin Prufer, Alicia Jo Rabins, Anna Duke Reach, Victoria Redel,
Martha Rhodes, Paula Rhodes, Louise Riemer, Sarah Santner,
Amy Schiffman, Peter and Jill Schireson, Roni and Richard Schotter,
James and Nancy Shalek, Soraya Shalforoosh, Peggy Shinner,
Anita Soos, Donna Spruijt-Metz, Ann F. Stanford, Arlene Stang,
Page Hill Starzinger, Marina Stuart, Yerra Sugarman, Marjorie and
Lew Tesser, Eleanor Thomas, Tom Thompson and Miranda Field,
James Tjoa, Ellen Bryant Voigt, Connie Voisine, Moira Walsh,
Ellen Dore Watson, Calvin Wei, John Wender, Eleanor Wilner,
Mary Wolf, and Pamela and Kelly Yenser.